THE
PASSION
TRANSLATION

THE PASSIONATE LIFE BIBLE STUDY SERIES

12-LESSON STUDY GUIDE

THE BOOK OF
JOHN
SECOND EDITION

ETERNAL LOVE

BroadStreet
PUBLISHING

BroadStreet Publishing® Group, LLC
Savage, Minnesota, USA
BroadStreetPublishing.com

TPT: The Book of John (2nd edition):
12-Lesson Bible Study Guide

978-1-4245-5909-1 (softcover)
978-1-4245-6076-9 (e-book)

Stock or custom editions of BroadStreet Publishing titles may be purchased in bulk for educational, business, ministry, fundraising, or sales promotional use. For information, please email info@broadstreetpublishing.com.

General editor: Dr. Brian Simmons
Managing editor: William D. Watkins
Contributing editors: W. Terry Whalin and Christy Phillippe
Writer: Christy Phillippe

Cover and interior by Garborg Design at GarborgDesign.com

Printed in the United States of America

20 21 22 23 24 5 4 3 2 1

CONTENTS

From God's Heart to Yours

"God is love," says the apostle John. "Everyone who loves is fathered by God and experiences an intimate knowledge of him" (1 John 4:7). The life of a Christ-follower is, at its core, a life of love—God's love of us, our love of him, and our love of others and ourselves because of God's love for us.

And this divine love is reliable, trustworthy, unconditional, other-centered, majestic, forgiving, redemptive, patient, kind, and more precious than anything else we can ever receive or give. It characterizes each person of the Trinity—Father, Son, and Holy Spirit—and is as unlimited as they are. They love one another with this eternal love, and they reach beyond themselves to us, created in their image with this love.

How do we know such incredible truths? Through the primary source of all else we know about the one God—his Word, the Bible. Of course, God reveals who he is through other sources as well, such as the natural world, miracles, our inner life, our relationships (especially with him), those who minister on his behalf, and those who proclaim him to us and others. But the fullest and most comprehensive revelation we have of God and from him is what he has given us in the thirty-nine books of the Hebrew Scriptures (the Old Testament) and the twenty-seven books of the Christian Scriptures (the New Testament). Together, these sixty-six books present a compelling and telling portrait of God and his dealings with us.

It is these Scriptures that *The Passionate Life Bible Study Series* is all about. Through these study guides, we—the editors and writers of this series—seek to provide you with a unique and welcoming opportunity to delve more deeply into God's precious Word, encountering there his loving heart for you and all the others he loves. God wants you to know him more deeply, to love him more devoutly, and to share his heart with others more frequently and freely. To accomplish this, we have based this study guide series on The Passion Translation of the Bible, which strives to "unlock the passion of [God's] heart." It is "a heart-level translation, from the passion of God's heart to the passion of your heart," created to "kindle in you a burning desire for him and his heart, while impacting the church for years to come."[1]

In each study guide, you will find an introduction to the Bible book it covers. There you will gain information about that Bible book's authorship, date of composition, first recipients, setting, purpose, central message, and key themes. Each lesson following the introduction will take a portion of that Bible book and walk you through it. You will learn its content better while experiencing and applying God's heart for your own life and encountering ways you can share his heart with others. Along the way, you will come across a number of features we have created that provide opportunities for more life application and growth in biblical understanding:

Experience God's Heart

This feature focuses questions on personal application. It will help you live out God's Word and bring the Bible into your world in fresh, exciting, and relevant ways.

Share God's Heart

This feature will help you grow in your ability to share with other people what you learn and apply in a given lesson. It provides guidance on how the lesson relates to growing closer to others, to enriching your fellowship with others. It also points the way to enabling you to better listen to the stories of others so you can bridge the biblical story with their stories.

The Backstory

This feature provides ancient historical and cultural background that illuminates Bible passages and teachings. It deals with then-pertinent religious groups, communities, leaders, disputes, business trades, travel routes, customs, nations, political factions, ancient measurements and currency . . . in short, anything historical or cultural that will help you better understand what Scripture says and means. You may also find maps and charts that will help you reimagine these groups, places, and activities. Finally, in this feature you will find references to additional Bible texts that will further illuminate the Scripture you are studying.

Word Wealth

This feature provides definitions and other illuminating information about key terms, names, and concepts and how different ancient languages have influenced the biblical text. It also provides insight into the different literary forms in the Bible, such as prophecy, poetry, narrative history, parables, and letters and how knowing the form of a text can help you better interpret and apply it. Finally, this feature highlights the most significant passages in a Bible book. You may be encouraged to memorize these verses or keep them before you in some way so you can actively hide God's Word in your heart.

Digging Deeper

This feature explains the theological significance of a text or the controversial issues that arise and mentions resources you can use to help you arrive at your own conclusions. Another way to dig deeper into the Word is by looking into the life of a biblical character or another person from church history, showing how that man or woman incarnated a biblical truth or passage. For instance, Jonathan Edwards was well known for his missions work among American Indians and for his intellectual prowess in articulating the Christian faith, Florence Nightingale for the reforms she brought about in healthcare, Irenaeus for his fight against heresy, Billy Graham for his work in evangelism, Moses for the strength God gave him to lead the Hebrews and receive and communicate the law, and Deborah for her work as a judge in Israel. This feature introduces to you figures from the past who model what it looks like to experience God's heart and share his heart with others.

The Extra Mile

While The Passion Translation's notes are extensive, sometimes students of Scripture like to explore more on their own. In this feature, we provide you with opportunities to glean more information from a Bible dictionary, a Bible encyclopedia, a reliable Bible online tool, another ancient text, and the like. Here you will learn how you can go the extra mile on a Bible lesson. And not just in study either. Reflection, prayer, discussion, and applying a passage in new ways provide even more opportunities to go the extra mile. Here you will find questions to answer and applications to make that will require more time and energy from you—if and when you have them to give.

As you can see above, each of these features has a corresponding icon so you can quickly and easily identify them.

You will find other help and guidance through the lessons of these study guides, including thoughtful questions, application suggestions, and spaces for you to record your own reflections, answers, and action steps. Of course, you can also write in your own journal, notebook, computer, or other resource, but we have provided you with space for your convenience.

Also, each lesson will direct you into the introductory material and numerous notes provided in The Passion Translation. There each Bible book contains a number of aids supplied to help you better grasp God's words and his incredible love, power, knowledge, plans, and so much more. We want you to get the most out of your Bible study, especially using it to draw you closer to the One who loves you most.

Finally, at the end of each lesson, you'll find a section called "Talking It Out." This contains questions and exercises for application that you can share, answer, and apply with your spouse, a friend, a coworker, a Bible study group, or any other individuals or groups who would like to walk with you through this material. As Christians, we gather together to serve, study, worship, sing, evangelize, and a host of other activities. We grow together, not just on our own. This section will give you ample opportunities to engage others with the content of each lesson so you can work it out in community.

We offer all of this to support you in becoming an even more faithful and loving disciple of Jesus Christ. A disciple in the ancient world was a student of her teacher, a follower of his master. Students study, and followers follow. Jesus' disciples are to sit at his feet and listen and learn and then do what he tells them and shows them to do. We have created *The Passionate Life Bible Study Series* to help you do what a disciple of Jesus is called to do.

So go.

Read God's words.

Hear what he has to say in them and through them.

Meditate on them.

Hide them in your heart.

Display their truth in your life.

Share their truths with others.

Let them ignite Jesus' passion and light in all you say and do.

Use them to help you fulfill what Jesus called his disciples to do: "'Now go in my authority and make disciples of all nations, baptizing them in the name of the Father, the Son, and the Holy Spirit. And teach them to faithfully follow all that I have commanded you. And never forget that I am with you every day, even to the completion of this age'" (Matthew 28:19–20).

And through all of this, let Jesus' love nourish your heart and allow that love to overflow into your relationships with others (John 15:9–13). For it was for love that Jesus came, served, died, rose from the dead, and ascended into heaven. This love he gives us. And this love he wants us to pass along to others.

Why I Love the Gospel of John

John is the apostle of love. His writings take us deeper into the love of God than perhaps any other author of the New Testament. John points us to the heart of God, not just to principles or events. His Gospel unveils mysteries of our faith and will show you things that will keep you pondering for the rest of your life. I know you'll love this study guide!

The very first book I read in the Bible after giving my life to Christ was the book of John. I was on a five-hour bus ride and decided I'd start reading the Bible. I flipped open to John's Gospel. I was gripped by the first words: "In the beginning was the Word and the Word was with God and the Word was God" (NIV).

Wow! Over the next few hours I devoured every word of John, stopping often to wipe away tears. By the end of the trip, I knew three things:

- God is real.

- Jesus is the only way to know God.

- God loves me.

These three truths will keep you strong through all the ups and downs of your life. God is so real, and his Word is so true! Jesus really will take you to the Father as his very own. And God loves you so dearly that he gave up his unique Son for you! John reveals these truths in so many ways, including by using the word *love* fifty-six times in his Gospel.

Another reason I love John is his focus on miracles. There are eight powerful miracles in the book of John, and each one shows us God's love and Jesus' power. These are the eight miracle-signs that will cause you to stop in your tracks and ponder the ways of God. They are a means to persuade us that Jesus is the true Messiah, the Son of God, and that we must believe *in him* to be saved:

- Water turned into wine (2:1–11)

- Healing of the royal official's son (4:46–54)

- Healing the paralytic at Bethesda (5:1–15)

- Feeding the multitudes (6:5–14)

- Walking on water (vv. 16–24)

- Healing the man blind from birth (9:1–7)

- Raising Lazarus from the dead (11:1–45)

- The resurrection of Jesus from the dead (20:1–31)

Each chapter of John will stir your heart. I encourage you to take an hour or more to be alone with God and read through the book of John, then go back and do this study and look over the powerful truths we've put inside just for you.

And may I suggest you spend some extra time with the lessons on the last week of Jesus' life, John 12–21. For me, John 19 is a chapter in the Bible that I come back to over and over. It describes the crucifixion and "passion" of the One we love.

You'll love studying John with me in the pages that follow. Thanks for being with us on this journey into the heart of God.

Dr. Brian Simmons
General Editor

The Beloved Disciple
and His Gospel

Welcome to the Gospel of John, one of the most profound portraits of Jesus the Christ shared in the entire Bible—yet also one of the most relatable.

In this Gospel, we will meet our Savior face-to-face, not just as a human being like we are but as God himself, the One who was present in ages past and who will reign throughout the ages to come.

The first three Gospels—Matthew, Mark, and Luke, otherwise known as the Synoptic Gospels due to their similarities—shine a spotlight on the things that Jesus did and the words that he taught. The Gospel of John is quite different. It moves beyond mere facts about Jesus' life on earth, focusing less on his activities and instead pulling back the curtain on who he really is, using spiritual and symbolic language and profound truths that point to Christ's divinity. The theological implications could not be greater: Jesus is God, and because he is, our salvation is secure.

But perhaps the greatest truth that can be discovered in this beautiful portrait of Christ is that *God loves you*. Arguably the most famous verse in the entire Bible is found within this book. John 3:16 gives us this simple yet life-changing good news: "For this is how much God loved the world—he gave his one and only, unique Son as a gift. So now everyone who believes in him will never perish but experience everlasting life." How breathtaking it is to realize that the very Son of God, who was present before and at the beginning of the universe and who will rule throughout eternity, was given—*to us*—as a gift, to offer us eternal light, life, and love!

Authorship

The Gospel of John was written by one of Jesus' closest friends. John was in Jesus' inner circle, one of his most passionate followers. John goes so far as to describe himself as "the disciple whom Jesus loved," an indication of not only their close relationship but also John's understanding of how his Savior truly felt about him. John had a unique revelation of God as love, and he was able to place himself squarely in the center of that love—the personal, passionate love that Jesus has for each of his followers and friends.

> Love unlocks mysteries. As we love Jesus,
> our hearts are unlocked to see more of his
> beauty and glory. When we stop defining
> ourselves by our failures, but rather as the
> one whom Jesus loves, then our hearts
> begin to open to the breathtaking discovery
> of the wonder of Jesus Christ.[2]

• *How would a greater understanding of your true identity—as "one whom Jesus loves"—change the way you view yourself? Be specific.*

- *List at least three ways you could relate to others differently in the light of Jesus' love for you and for them.*

Date of Composition

It is likely that the Gospel of John was written only a few decades after Jesus' death and resurrection, which most scholars believe took place between 30 and 33 CE. (The abbreviations "CE" and "BCE"—meaning "of the Common Era" and "Before the Common Era"—are used here to denote the year-numbering system that relates to the Gregorian calendar in use throughout the world today. They correlate to the same eras indicated by the abbreviations "AD" and "BC," but they are a more common international standard in our time.)

- *How might this make John's account of Jesus' life and ministry more reliable than if it had been written many more decades later?*

Recipients of the Gospel

John wrote this passionate account of Jesus' life, death, and resurrection to convince unbelievers that the eternal Son of God had come to save them from their sins. Jesus not only gives life; he is *the* Life. Jesus not only gives light; he is *the* Light. And John was also writing to believers to convince them to walk more fully in the life and the light of their loving Savior.

- *How are you, as one of John's readers today, approaching the study of this account of Jesus' life? Are you skeptical, not fully convinced of Jesus' claims but seeking truth and meaning in your life? Or are you already a wholehearted, passionate believer, eager to soak in more of Jesus' life, light, and love through this study? Or maybe you're just curious, wondering what this book says about Jesus of Nazareth? What is your frame of mind and heart situation as you come to this study?*

- *What do you hope to get out of the Gospel of John?*

# WORD WEALTH

A key passage in this Gospel comes toward the end of it:

> Jesus went on to do many more miraculous
> signs in the presence of his disciples,
> which are not even included in this book.
> But all that is recorded here is so that you
> will fully believe that Jesus is the Anointed
> One, the Son of God, and that through your
> faith in him you will experience eternal life
> by the power of his name! (20:30–31)

As you can see from this important passage in John's account of Jesus' life, a key word throughout this Gospel is *believe*. In the Greek, this word is *episteuo*, and it goes beyond a mere intellectual assent. It involves a passionate surrender—an unwavering trust—in the person of Jesus and in the work he has done for your salvation.

- *Has your belief in Jesus, the Son of God, moved beyond a mental agreement with what the Bible says about him and into a deep, abiding, trust relationship? If so, tell the story of how that happened.*

- *How has that belief transformed your life?*

Setting and Purpose

John wrote his Gospel at a time when the early church was spreading the good news of salvation to both Jews and Gentiles. John's purpose is explicitly stated in the key verse: He wrote these words *for you.* He wants *you* to believe in Jesus as the Son of God so that you will receive the eternal life that Jesus now offers.

Key Themes

John weaves several primary themes throughout his Gospel: the person and the work of Jesus Christ, the salvation that Jesus brings to the world, the Holy Spirit who empowers believers in Jesus to live out his teachings, and the end of the age, when Jesus himself will come again to right all that is wrong and establish his everlasting kingdom.

- *Which of these themes most resonates with you at the beginning of this study? Why?*

The Core Message

John's central message comes through the most well-known verse from his Gospel, chapter 3, verse 16. There John capsulizes that Jesus, as the Son of God and a walking, talking demonstration of God's love, brings the light and life of salvation to the world.

♥ EXPERIENCE GOD'S HEART

- *Reread John 3:16 in The Passion Translation. Although it's a familiar verse to many of us, its truths are eternal. Has the deep revelation of how much God loves you—as an individual, as his unique creation—changed how you look at yourself up to this point in our study? If so, in what ways?*

- *Now read on to verse 17 in chapter 3. Jesus came not to judge and condemn the world but to rescue it. In what ways do you need rescuing today? In what ways can you allow Jesus to be your Savior in those areas?*

❤ SHARE GOD'S HEART

John experienced a deeply intimate and passionate relationship with Jesus, and he wrote his Gospel to introduce his close friend to as many other people as he could. He couldn't keep the good news to himself!

- *How willing are you to share the good news of your own personal relationship with Jesus with those around you?*

- *Do you ever hesitate, perhaps out of fear of rejection or a sense of embarrassment? If so, what might be holding you back?*

- *John's experience with Jesus changed his life. How has your own experience with Jesus changed your life? With whom can you share this experience today? Who most needs to know the change an encounter with the Savior can bring?*

Talking It Out

Since Christians grow in community, not just in solitude, here are some questions you may want to discuss with another person or in a group. Each "Talking It Out" section is designed with this purpose in mind.

1. At the time of the events in the book of John, the Jewish people were eager for and expecting a political Messiah to save them from Roman oppression. Jesus came on the scene as their Savior—but not the Savior they were expecting. How can our expectations skew or inform our perspective of events?

2. How has knowing Jesus met or exceeded your own expectations? How is the hope he offers different from what the world might be searching for?

3. How does the salvation that Jesus offers give us what we *need* and not just what we *want*? How does this play out on a practical level in people's lives? In your own?

4. Certain themes run throughout the Gospel of John. Two of these are *light* and *life*. How is Jesus both light and life to our world, which needs both so desperately?

5. How can we, as individuals and corporately, offer light and life to the hurting people around us?

LESSON 1

Jesus, the Living Expression of God

(1:1–18)

"Sticks and stones . . . " Do you remember that saying about your words from when you were a kid? It implied that words don't really count. But today we know that's not the case. Our words are important.

Our words carry meaning.

Our words carry weight.

Our words carry promises and intent.

Our words are an expression of who we are, what we think, and how we feel.

Many believe that the first eighteen verses of John's Gospel are an ancient hymn of the early church. It is a sacred poem that paints a beautiful picture of who Jesus really is. He is the very *Word* of God, the Living Expression of the Father's heart.

Just as you express your own thoughts, hopes, dreams, and desires—your very self—by the words you choose to speak, God sent Jesus, his Son, who was in all ways divine just as he was, to express himself and *his* thoughts, hopes, and dreams for his lost children on the earth.

The Gospel of John is the story of that Living Expression's life and work among us.

🅗 WORD WEALTH

The word *logos* comes from ancient Greek philosophy, and it refers to an impersonal force, the reason and order and purpose present and necessary for our universe to exist. In Hebrew thinking, however, the *logos* becomes personal, referring to Yahweh, the Creator who set the universe into motion and even now gives it unity, cohesion, logic, and purpose.

This is the word that the beloved disciple chose to use to describe Jesus as the Living Expression of God himself. No English word really comes close to fully communicating its meaning. Some have tried to translate *logos*, rather ineffectively, into the English words *logic*, *reason*, and even *act* or *deed*.

The Word seems to come the closest to capturing its multifaceted meaning. Jesus is the full expression of God's character, power, and love—but he also adds the element of action, purpose, and deed. He expresses who God is, and he lives that out before us.

That this Word became a human being like us and lived among us on the earth—that is the startling premise of John's Gospel. The God of eons past and of the everlasting future was so crazy-passionate about his children that he made a radical move to show us his love. That's what this Living Expression is all about.

"In the Very Beginning"

John 1:2 refers to this Living Expression—Jesus—being with God "in the very beginning." Do those words sound familiar? John is quite different from the other three Gospel writers, who all chose to begin their accounts at Jesus' earthly birth or the beginning of his ministry. John asserts that, in fact, Jesus *had no beginning*— that he has always been present, face-to-face with God as part of the Godhead, present and active in creation since the beginning of time. John says that this Living Expression was and is "fully God" (v. 1).

- *We often think of Jesus as being a man who was born as a baby to Mary and Joseph and who walked this earth two thousand years ago. What comes to mind when you realize that he was present and active at the creation of the world? That he existed even before that—into eternity past—as the divine Son of God? Reflect on his deity, eternal existence, creative power, and ability to incarnate as a human being. Record your thoughts and even praise and worship.*

🔟 WORD WEALTH

The prologue to John's Gospel was likely a hymn of the early church, an ancient poem written for Christians to use in their worship of Jesus as the eternal God who came to earth as a man to show us what the Father was really like. Its beautiful, mysterious, and poetic language has survived thousands of years, and we now hold it in our hands today.

- *Why not join your voice with the voices of believers throughout the ages who have sung this hymn? Read these verses (1:1–18) aloud in praise to Jesus today, even sing them if you like.*

 DIGGING DEEPER

Jesus: Good Man or the God-Man?

The Gospel of John has, as one of its main focuses, the fact that Jesus is God.

A popular belief held by many people today is that Jesus was just a good man who lived and died two thousand years ago. The famous Christian apologist C. S. Lewis once called this idea preposterous. He noted that Jesus called himself God, so he was either lying (and therefore *not* a "good man"), or he was a lunatic (since he ultimately allowed himself to be crucified over these claims), or he is the divine Lord.

- *Which of these three conclusions have you arrived at? Explain the process you went through to come to this conclusion.*

- *Why is it so important for our salvation that Jesus be more than a mere human being? Why must he be God himself to be able to save us?*

Recognizing Him and Receiving Him

The beloved disciple went on to write these words:

> He [the Living Expression] came to the very
> people he created—to those who should have
> recognized him, but they did not receive him.
> (v. 11)

- *In what ways have you failed to recognize Jesus in your life?*

- *In what ways have you failed to receive him in your life?*

• *List three ways in which you can recognize his work and receive more of him on this day in the situations you are facing right now.*

🎞 THE BACKSTORY

God has always longed to be close to his people, but a barrier created by sin kept them from his presence. In the Old Testament, the tabernacle was constructed before a permanent temple was built. This tabernacle traveled with God's people throughout the wilderness, and deep within its walls, behind a thick cloth barrier, God's very presence inhabited the holy of holies. It was as close as he could get to his beloved children—until Jesus came on the scene.

The Living Expression "became a man and lived among us" (1:14), which literally means that "he pitched his tent among us." Jesus is God's literal presence with us, in the midst of us, living with us in much the same way that God once came down to the earth within the confines of the tabernacle.

And at the moment of Jesus' death on the cross, the temple veil that kept sinful human beings away from God's presence in the holy of holies was literally ripped in two—from top to bottom (Matthew 27:51). Jesus not only shows us what God is really like, but he has also opened up the way for us to get to know the Father for ourselves.

 WORD WEALTH

Later in John's Gospel, Jesus tells his disciples that he is the Way, the Truth, and the Life (14:6). In the Prologue of his Gospel, John introduces us to the revelation that Jesus is truth embodied in human flesh:

> And so the Living Expression
> became a man and lived among us!
> And we gazed upon the splendor of his glory,
> the glory of the One and Only
> who came from the Father overflowing
> with tender mercy and truth! . . .
> Moses gave us the Law, but Jesus,
> the Anointed One,
> unveils truth wrapped in tender mercy. (1:14, 17)

Jesus is truth. So many times, we want justice and truth—for others.

Jesus is mercy. So many times, we want mercy and forgiveness—for ourselves.

- *How are these observations true in what you see in the world around you?*

- *In your own life?*

 # THE EXTRA MILE

- *In what ways can you invite Jesus to be both truth and mercy in every area of your life and world? Be specific.*

 # EXPERIENCE GOD'S HEART

> And this Living Expression is the Light that bursts through gloom—the Light that darkness could not diminish! (1:5)

To many people, the world seems to be a gloomier place today than it was years ago. Political bickering, economic troubles, domestic terrorism, the threat of global war, and unspeakable violence all fill the nightly news broadcasts.

- *What most overwhelms you about the world we live in today?*

What's going on around us doesn't even take into account the personal challenges that each of us faces on a daily basis—bills, health issues, relationship problems, job issues, and loss. The list of problems that we face sometimes seems endless.

- *Have any parts of your life brought you into a place of darkness and gloom? If so, what are they?*

- *Do you still feel stuck in those places or have you been able to move beyond them, even partly? If the former, what have you tried to pull yourself out of those dark situations? If the latter, what did you do that enabled you to overcome?*

Sometimes it seems as though the dark things we face are certain to bring us down, to "diminish" us in some way. But Jesus is the Light that cannot be diminished by *any* form of darkness.

- *In the space below, list a "dark" or difficult situation you are facing, then list the ways you have feared it might diminish you. Finally, consider the ways in which Jesus can bring—and is bringing—his light and life into the situation, dispelling the gloom.*

For example:
<u>Situation:</u> My husband just handed me divorce papers.
<u>How it might diminish me:</u> I am afraid I am losing my family.
<u>How Jesus dispels the gloom:</u> Jesus promises to never leave me or forsake me. He will see me through this, and I will never be alone.

Now it's your turn:

 THE EXTRA MILE

- *John tells us that Jesus is the Light that bursts through gloom. What amazing news! List three or four ways you have seen Jesus burst through the gloom in your own life in the last few weeks.*

- *List three or four ways you have seen Jesus recently burst through gloom in the world.*

❤ SHARE GOD'S HEART

Meet John the Baptist (the messenger, not the beloved disciple who wrote the Gospel):

> For he came to be a witness, to point the way to
> the Light of Life, and to help everyone believe.
> John was not that Light but he came to show
> who is.
> For he was merely a messenger to speak the
> truth about the Light. (1:7–8)

- *List three ways in which you are currently a witness of the Light to those around you.*

- *Who are five people in your life or your community who need a greater glimpse of this Light in their lives? In what practical and loving ways could you be a witness of Jesus' light, life, and love to them this week?*

John makes it clear that the messenger (John the Baptist) was *not* the Light himself. However, it can be easy to point out the sins and faults of others as we speak to them and set ourselves in the place of God, even when we are trying to share the light of Jesus.

- *Have you ever been guilty of this? If so, tell the story. What was the outcome?*

- *Consider how you can better step back and let God do his own work in people's lives as you point the way to Jesus. What are your thoughts?*

Conclusion

Have you ever experienced a birthday or Christmas or other special occasion when someone went over and beyond to shower you with extravagance? So much so that you felt like saying, "Enough! I don't deserve all of this!"? John tells us that we have received from God "grace heaped upon more grace" (v. 16). The word *grace* literally means "gift" or "present."

- *What feelings move through you when you think about how extravagantly God loves you?*

- *How have you received "gifts upon more gifts" from him throughout the years? Record as many examples as you can.*

John 1:18 tells us: "No one has ever gazed upon the fullness of God's splendor except the uniquely beloved Son, who is cherished by the Father and held close to his heart."

- *Jesus came to earth from the closest place of intimacy with the Father God. What does this say to you about how God the Father feels about his children?*

- *About you personally?*

Talking It Out

1. In John 1:1–5, we are told a number of facts about the "Living Expression" of God—Jesus. List as many of these facts as you can. Which of them helps you relate the most to this Living Expression?

2. Read John 1:12. What does it mean to receive Jesus, and what is the result? Do you think everyone in your church knows Jesus this way? If not, what are some ways you and others in your church can lead people there to embrace Jesus?

3. Read Isaiah 7:14 and then read John 1:14. How does the New Testament passage fulfill the Old? In what other ways has Jesus fulfilled promises given in the Old Testament?

4. What does it mean to you to realize that our God is a promise-keeping God? What promises to you has he kept? Which promises are you still waiting for him to fulfill?

LESSON 2

The Lion Turned Lamb

(1:19–51)

When God promised his people a savior, the people largely misunderstood him. For centuries before Jesus' birth, the prophets wrote of the arrival of the Son of God and the Living Expression of his heart toward his children, who was eternally present with the Father and eternally God himself. But human expectation painted his entrance into human history in the form of the Lion of Judah. John, our Gospel writer, also wrote about this Lion in another book of the Bible (see Revelation 5).

There is no doubt that Jesus will return to earth someday as that strong and powerful, victorious Lion, but in his first coming to our sin-plagued planet, the Son willingly set aside his power and might and instead took on the nature of the meek and humble Lamb of God.

Who is this Lamb who approaches John the Messenger asking to be baptized in the Jordan River?

Let's move in closer to find out for ourselves.

DIGGING DEEPER

John the Baptist

Many readers of the Gospel of John reach verse 19 of chapter 1, and when they encounter the name "John," they assume this is the same person whose book they are reading. This is not the case.

As we discovered in lesson 1, the Gospel of John was written by the "beloved disciple," one who loved Jesus passionately and who couldn't wait to tell the world about him by writing down his experiences and encounters with Jesus during the three years of friendship and ministry that they shared.

It is a different John—John the Baptist—who bursts on the scene toward the end of chapter 1 of the Beloved's Gospel. This John also could not keep the good news of Jesus to himself, but he took a different approach. God's call compelled him to set up camp by the Jordan River and begin imploring the people he met there to change their ways, to prepare themselves for an imminent encounter with the very Son of God.

Here's the interesting part: Jesus and John were actually cousins, from the very same family, born just a few months apart. They played together as children and likely saw each other in the synagogue schools, at temple functions, and at the frequent family get-togethers in which Jewish families of that era typically participated.

To John, Jesus had likely been there for as long as he could remember. He was the oldest son in Mary and Joseph's brood, one of the cousins whom John might have chased through the carpenter shop when they were kids.

But at some point something changed.

At some point, the sandals of the younger cousin who had once played ball with John in the dusty streets became the sandals that John was not worthy enough to even stoop down and untie. At some point, the understanding of who Jesus really was dawned upon John's consciousness—and it turned his life upside down.

He couldn't keep the news to himself.

• *At what point did the revelation of who Jesus really is dawn upon you?*

• *How did it transform your life?*

• *In what ways were you then compelled to share that news with other people?*

THE BACKSTORY

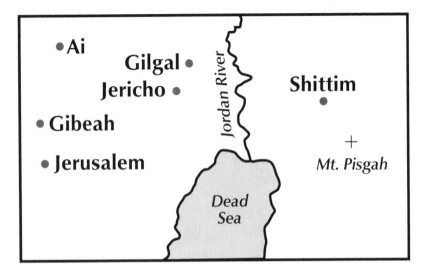

John was baptizing near the very spot on the banks of the Jordan River where God's people had crossed over into their promised land many centuries before. That day had brought a new beginning for God's cherished children as they fully walked into the fulfillment of his promise to them. Jesus brought this full circle when he presented himself—God's ultimate promise kept—to be baptized in the very same location.

The Lamb of God Has Arrived

The people of Israel were familiar with lambs for the sacrifices. At Passover, each family had to have a lamb, and during the year, two lambs a day were sacrificed at the temple altar, plus all the other lambs brought for personal sacrifices. Those lambs were brought by people to people, but here is God's Lamb, given by God to humankind! Those lambs could not take away sin, but the Lamb of God can take away sin. Those lambs were for Israel alone, but this Lamb would shed His blood for the whole world![3]

Jesus—the Lion, the Light, the Life of God—makes his grand entrance into John's Gospel in the meekest way possible. He willingly set aside his power and took on the role of an animal led to be sacrificed in our place. And John the Baptist cries out his passionate introduction, not of the cousin he'd known since childhood, but of the sinless Savior of the world: "Look! There he is—God's Lamb!" (1:29).

• *What do these words of John the Baptist mean to you?*

• *To whom do you need to declare that same message to today? Make a plan to point that person to God's Lamb, Jesus, as soon as possible.*

John not only pointed to Jesus as God's Lamb, but he also described what Jesus would do—his mission on the earth: "He will take away the sin of the world!" (v. 29).

> The Aramaic is, "the sins of the universe."
> To take away our sins is a figure of speech that means "he will break sin's grip from humanity, taking away both its guilt and power from those who believe."[4]

• *Have you ever considered what it means for Jesus to take away your sins? Record your thoughts.*

• *Jesus' taking away your sins could involve helping you to resist future temptations. What temptations do you currently face? How would Jesus' taking away your sins in this way make a difference in your life?*

• *Jesus' taking away your sins could also involve removing the guilt of your past. What guilt are you currently carrying from wrongs you may have done? (They could be from yesterday or from decades ago.) How would Jesus' taking away your sins in this way make a difference in your life?*

The Lamb and the Dove

Jesus, the Lamb, took away our sins, and the Holy Spirit, the Dove, brings to man the life of God. Jesus didn't come to start a movement, but to bring the fullness of life to us. This "Dove" points to the dove that Noah released from the ark. It found no place to rest in a fallen world. The last time Noah released the dove it flew and never returned. It flew throughout history over Abraham and the patriarchs, over the prophets and kings with no place to rest, until at last, there was a heavenly man who carried the life of heaven—upon him the dove (Holy Spirit) rested and remained. There was nothing that could offend heaven in the life of our Lord Jesus.[5]

- *Read John 1:32. What does it mean that the Spirit of God rested on Jesus "from that moment forward"?*

 THE EXTRA MILE

- *The same writer of this Gospel, John, wrote of Jesus' baptism and the Spirit's work in 1 John 5:6–9. Read these verses. What is the work of the Spirit that is mentioned?*

- *How has the Holy Spirit revealed Jesus to you?*

- *What difference has it made?*

- *In what ways can you invite this Dove to rest and remain more fully in your life?*

♥ EXPERIENCE GOD'S HEART

In the latter part of John 1, Jesus began calling his first followers: Andrew, Simon, Philip, and Nathanael. When Jesus encountered Andrew and his brother Simon, whom Jesus would later call Peter the Rock, he asked them a very important question: "What do you want?" (v. 38).

- *What about you? What did you want when you first started following Jesus?*

- *Were those expectations met? If so, how?*

- *What do you want from Jesus today?*

- *Are there any limits to how far you would follow Jesus? If so, what are they? What can you do to break those limits so you can follow him passionately wherever he leads?*

Nathanael's Moment of Shock and Awe

We toss around the phrase "shock and awe" these days when something is so impressive that we find it hard to believe. Nathanael experienced this when Jesus was able to tell him where he was and what he was doing at a certain time in the not-too-distant past. It might have been a bit like our amazement when someone performs a good magic trick or sleight of hand that we just can't figure out.

But Jesus says, "Wait—you haven't seen *anything* yet!" Take a look at his response:

> Jesus answered, "Do you believe simply because I told you I saw you sitting under a fig tree? You will experience even more impressive things than that! I prophesy to you eternal truth: From now on you will see an open heaven and gaze upon the Son of Man like a Stairway reaching into the sky with the messengers of God climbing up and down upon him!" (vv. 50–51)

 THE BACKSTORY

Jacob's Ladder

Take a few minutes to read the account of Jacob's ladder recorded in Genesis 28.

It seems clear that Jesus had this encounter with Jacob in mind when he spoke the words recorded in John 1:50–51.

- *Why do you think Jesus chose to refer to this Old Testament account?*

Some Bible scholars believe that it was the pre-incarnate Son of God who wrestled with Jacob those many hundreds of years before, not too long after Jacob's vision of the stairway to heaven (see Genesis 32). Perhaps Jesus the Son was fondly remembering his encounters with God's people as he made the point that he himself was the Stairway—the bridge between a holy God in heaven and his sinful children on the earth.

- *How does this idea inform your understanding of what Jesus was saying to Nathanael—and to you—in this passage?*

❤ SHARE GOD'S HEART

You can almost see the sides of Jesus' mouth twitch in amusement and anticipation. Nathanael was already amazed that Jesus could tell him where he had been and what he had been doing at a certain time of day. Imagine Jesus' newest follower's reactions as the rest of Jesus' life, death, and resurrection unfolded. *What would happen next?* Nathanael may have wondered.

- *What did Jesus promise that Nathanael would experience? (See John 1:50.)*

- *How mind-blown do you think Nathanael was when he heard those words? What do you think his reaction would have been?*

- *What would have been your reaction if you had been in Nathanael's sandals on that day?*

- *What is the most impressive thing that God has ever done in your life? Tell the story.*

- *Name some people who might need to hear your particular story today.*

- *What would be some effective ways to go about sharing with these people God's impressive work in your life as soon as possible? Feel free to be creative.*

Talking It Out

1. This week we met another John in the narrative of Jesus' life—not the writer of the Gospel but John the Baptizer, Jesus' cousin and the one who proclaimed Jesus' identity and arrival. What was his testimony concerning Jesus? What results did he see?

2. How did John the Baptizer point people away from himself and toward Jesus? How can you follow his example in this focus on the Savior?

3. In John 1:35–51, the reactions of five different people to Jesus are recorded. What responses most resonate with you? Which responses to Jesus have you seen in other people? In yourself?

LESSON 3

Turning the World Upside Down

(2:1-4:42)

Jesus, the Living Expression of God, has finally arrived on the scene—and he is far different from anyone's expectations. Many of the religious people of Jesus' day were actively watching for a savior, but the savior they expected was a political leader to free them from Roman rule and oppression. Jesus, however, hadn't come to earth to save them in a temporary political or societal way; he brought eternal salvation—opening the way to reconnect with God and enjoy eternal life with him in heaven.

Still today, Jesus continues to defy our religious expectations. Where we expect God's condemnation and judgment, Jesus comes to say, *God is full of love and grace. You can be forgiven.* And where we may expect God to turn a blind eye to the wrongs around us, especially those to which we have grown accustomed, Jesus passionately defends the cause of justice and truth. The Son of God has come to show us the Father, and as he does, he continues to turn the world upside down.

- *What kinds of preconceptions have you held of God that a deeper relationship with Jesus has transformed? Jot down some notes on how these changes took place.*

Weddings, Water, and Wine

When Jesus' mother, Mary, approached him with the problem of a shortage of wine at a family wedding, she said, in essence:

> "Religion has failed; it has run out of wine." The traditions of religion cannot gladden the heart, but Jesus can. Moses (the Law) turned water into blood, but Jesus (grace) turned water into wine.[6]

- *Name some religious traditions you have followed in the past or still follow today.*

- *Why do you follow them? Is it a matter of simple rote or habit, or do these traditions reach down to your heart? If so, in what ways?*

- *Can religious traditions better enhance your relationship with Jesus? If so, how?*

When Jesus changed the water into wine, he impressed the master of ceremonies with its quality and taste. In fact, this same gentleman told the bridegroom, "Every host serves his best wine first until everyone has had a cup or two, then he serves the wine of poor quality. But you, my friend, you've reserved the most exquisite wine until now!" (John 2:10).

Jesus set a precedent with his first miracle here—that he loves to shower his friends with good things, giving them with joyful abandon. The bridegroom went from having no wine at all—meaning certain humiliation—to receiving compliments on serving the best wine in town—all thanks to Jesus' extravagant generosity.

- *How about you? Has there ever been a time when you went from having less than nothing to blessed beyond measure thanks to a miracle from the Lord? Tell about it.*

- *How does this miracle inspire you to believe for even greater blessings from God in the future?*

Overturning the Tables

While Jesus' first miracle at Cana of Galilee demonstrated the extravagant grace of our God, the Lord's next encounter recorded in the Gospel of John exemplified his sense of extravagant truth and justice.

In the temple, where the people purchased animals to be sacrificed so they could temporarily cover their sins and be made right with a holy God, Jesus discovered egregious sins being committed: Those selling the animals and those exchanging currency for the temple tax were vastly overcharging the people in order to line their own pockets! The Son of God was outraged. He found some rope and created a whip, then drove the corrupt merchants out of his Father's house.

As they witnessed the Master's actions, the disciples were reminded of the words of King David in Psalm 69:9: "I am consumed with a fiery passion to keep your house pure!" (John 2:17).

• *Many people picture Jesus as a meek and humble man, a loving Savior willing to accept sinners—and their sin. How does this account of Jesus turning over tables in the temple counter that idea?*

• *Jesus was consumed by a "fiery passion" when he encountered sin—and he took action. Is there any sin in your life to which he might also react in this way? If so, what is it?*

- *What can you do to tap in to his fiery passion to rid your life of these things?*

- *The people had grown so accustomed to the exorbitant temple monetary charges that these charges likely seemed like just another thing to put up with in daily life. Jesus passionately disagreed. What cultural trends do you see that Jesus might confront today with his fiery passion of truth and justice?*

- *Are there ways in which you could align yourself with Jesus' stance against these cultural sins? What can you do to help demonstrate God's extravagant grace and his decisive truth in the world around you?*

A Midnight Visitor

In the middle of the night, a member of the Jewish ruling council and a sect called the Pharisees paid a visit to Jesus. Nicodemus had questions about the miracles that Jesus was performing, and he wanted to know where Jesus' abilities came from. He was afraid to approach Jesus during the day because of what his religious colleagues might think. Instead, he approached Jesus "discreetly" (John 3:2).

- *Have you ever wanted to hide your relationship with Jesus or your interest in the things of God? From whom were you hiding it? Why? What was the result?*

 EXPERIENCE GOD'S HEART

In Cana of Galilee, Jesus surprised the people with his gracious miracle of changing water into wine. In the temple, he shocked the crowds with his violent confrontation of sin. And in the third chapter of John's Gospel, he turned the thinking of Nicodemus completely upside down.

> Jesus answered, "I speak an eternal truth: Unless you are born of water and Spirit-wind, you will never enter God's kingdom realm. For the natural realm can only give

birth to things that are natural, but the
spiritual realm gives birth to supernatural
life!" (3:5–6)

Nicodemus was confused about this new kind of birth. Jesus explained further in what is arguably the most well-known verse of the Bible, John 3:16: "For this is how much God loved the world—he gave his one and only, unique Son as a gift. So now everyone who believes in him will never perish but experience everlasting life." This is the greatest news anyone could ever receive! These verses go hand in hand with the words of John the Baptist that we read at the end of this chapter: "Those who trust in the Son possess eternal life; but those who don't obey the Son will not see life, and God's anger will rise up against them" (v. 36).

- *What special meaning, if any, has John 3:16 had in your spiritual journey thus far?*

- *One of the potential translations of John 3:16 is that "God proved he loved the world by giving his Son."[7] Has God successfully proved this to you? If so, how?*

♥ SHARE GOD'S HEART

As Jesus passed through the region of Samaria, he grew thirsty, and he and his disciples stopped at a well in the heat of the day, hoping for a drink. When a woman from the nearby village came to get water, Jesus asked her for a drink.

> The "water" Jesus wanted was the refreshing, satisfying pleasure of her devotion. He says to each one of us, "Nothing satisfies me except you." The sinner drank of the Savior and the Savior drank of the sinner and both were satisfied. Neither ate or drank, but both were satisfied.[8]

- *Picture the Savior speaking these words to you: "Nothing satisfies me but you." Write your response to this heartfelt statement of Jesus.*

Eventually Jesus' love and grace touched the heart of the Samaritan woman. Again, he was full of surprises as he told the woman her very own life story (4:16–18).

Although the woman initially responded with an intellectual discussion about where and how God should be worshiped, Jesus soon made a dramatic disclosure of his true identity: "The Anointed One is here speaking with you—I am the One you're looking for" (v. 26).

- *What did the woman do next? (Read John 4:28–30.)*

- *When was the last time you dropped everything to run and tell what Jesus did for you?*

- *What sparked your enthusiasm then?*

- *What was the result?*

The Samaritan woman was probably well known in her village—and not in a good way. With five failed marriages, she might not at first glance seem to us to be an "ideal" representative of Jesus' message. But her honest confession and the measure of grace the Savior showed her actually made her the perfect witness. She could point others to Jesus in a way no one else could.

- *What past sins or failures have held you back from sharing the love and the heart of Jesus with those around you?*

- *How can you proudly introduce others to the man who knows "everything you've ever done"—and who loves you still?*

Jesus compares people who still need to come to know the love of the Father as part of a "great harvest." One of his greatest statements that encourage us to share his life, light, and love is this: "Look at all the people coming—now is harvest time! . . . And everyone who reaps these souls for eternal life will receive a reward" (vv. 35–36).

- *Who are the people in your life whose souls are ready to "be reaped for eternal life"?*

Talking It Out

1. What does it mean to be "born again" or experience the "rebirth"? What fundamental changes does this experience make in our standing with the Father? And in how we live from day to day?

2. In what ways can you relate to the woman at the well? In what ways has Jesus met you at the point of your need? Tell the story.

3. Like Jesus' first followers, Nicodemus, and the woman at the well, many people have misconceptions of who Jesus really is. What are some of these faulty ideas? In each case, what can you point out that would correct that misunderstanding? In other words, what can you say to clear the way to the true Jesus and away from a mischaracterization of who he is and what he came to do?

LESSON 4

Believing in Jesus

(4:43–5:47)

As kids, we may have "believed" in Santa Claus, the tooth fairy, or any number of other childhood fantasies that, as we grew older, we realized were not actually true.

So when we are asked as adults to believe in God or believe in Jesus, we may have wondered about the reality of what we were now supposed to believe in. It may have also raised questions about what belief in something really involves. What is the difference between believing in a fantasy and believing in something that's a fact? What does it mean to actually believe in something or someone? Does it mean that you intellectually agree, that you mentally assent to the reality of that thing or person? Does it mean that you consider that person to be telling the truth about what he or she is claiming?

Historic Christianity has long taught that to believe in Jesus involves much more than just nodding your head in agreement; it is more than just an intellectual assent to what Jesus said or did. True belief in Jesus involves agreeing with what he said and did *and* changing our lives accordingly. Jesus wants us to take action, to actually do something with our belief. It's one thing to nod our heads and say we agree with Jesus; it's a whole other thing to put his way into practice in our lives.

As we dig deeper into the Gospel of John, Jesus begins to lay a foundation for what it means to genuinely believe in him. He starts with addressing the official in Capernaum whose son was extremely sick, he continues when he heals a man just inside the city of Jerusalem, and then he makes his points very clear as he discusses his earthly mission with the Jewish leaders of his day. Let's take a look.

The Capernaum Official's Son

When Jesus returned to Cana of Galilee, he encountered a government official whose son was very ill to the point that he was about to die. When the man met up with Jesus, he begged him to go to Capernaum with him, where his son was, so that Jesus might touch his son and heal him.

- *What miracle had Jesus already performed in Cana of Galilee?*

- *It is possible that word of this miracle had gotten out. Would this have made believing in Jesus' ability to work miracles any easier? Why or why not?*

- *When the man from Capernaum made his plea to Jesus, how did Jesus respond? What did he say? (See John 4:48.)*

- *Close your eyes and picture Jesus uttering these words. What do you think his mood was? Frustration? Exasperation? Understanding and acceptance?*

- *What would his attitude be if he were uttering those words to you today concerning a miracle you are praying for in your own life?*

The truth is, Jesus meets each of us where we are at—physically, emotionally, and spiritually. And in his great compassion, he healed the man's son. Jesus loved the people to whom he had been sent. Their deep concerns were his.

- *What happened when Jesus healed the man's son? (Read John 4:50.)*

- *At what point did you believe in Jesus? Was your belief based on signs, wonders, and miracles you had seen performed in Jesus' name? What influenced you to accept him by faith?*

- *Return to the historical account in John 4. Who believed as a result of this miracle? (Read John 4:53–54.)*

The Pool at Bethesda

After Jesus healed the Capernaum official's son in the village of Cana of Galilee, he traveled to Jerusalem, where he entered the main gate and approached the pool at Bethesda.

🅗 WORD WEALTH

The word *hesed* means "loving-kindness"—a form of God's grace that he gives us unconditionally. The place name *Bethesda* therefore means "house of loving-kindness."[9] It is fitting that Jesus performed one of his greatest healing miracles at the pool located in the "house of God's loving-kindness." Jesus came to show us what the Father is like, and the Father's loving-kindness overflows from his throne onto his people. He longs to bless each of us with healing, brought to us in the life-giving waters of his grace.

- *God's house is one of loving-kindness. If you were to name your own household, what would it be? Why?*

Before Jesus came on the scene, the healings that took place at the pool of Bethesda were based entirely on works—the ability of the individual to get into the water in time to be eligible to receive the miracle being offered. But when Jesus arrived, he didn't even bother to consider the repercussions of helping the man who needed healing. And he didn't make the man find a way to get into the pool himself. He was the healer. He did the work.

The same is true for you: Jesus has done all the work for *your* salvation and healing—whether in this life or in the next—if you will only believe. Belief is what makes all the difference.

- *Consider your relationship with Jesus. In what ways are you still trying to "do the work" for your own salvation? For your own healing? To get your prayers answered?*

- *Jesus is more interested in a relationship with you than he is in any good works you could try to perform. You don't need to earn his favor; you already have it. What does this mean for your relationship with God?*

- *What changes would a deeper realization of this make in your life?*

 EXPERIENCE GOD'S HEART

When Jesus walked up to the crippled man by the pool, he knew that the man had been there for many years. The man had a reason: He had been entirely unable to get in the pool in time to receive healing. His crippled body was to blame, causing a vicious cycle of pain and disappointment that had continued for decades.

- *What strange question did Jesus ask this crippled man in John 5:6?*

- *Many people would think the answer to this question would be obvious. Why do you think Jesus asked the man this particular question?*

- *What need do you currently have in your own life? Maybe it's a need for healing, like this man was experiencing. Maybe you need God to move in some other way. Write out here the ways in which you need God to come through for you.*

- *Now consider how badly you want this particular need to be met. Jesus asks you the same question: Do you long to be healed? What difference would it make in your life? To what lengths would you go to get it?*

- *Jesus freely offers healing. He intervened in the crippled man's life at the pool of Bethesda, and he stands willing to intervene in your life today. But once he has intervened, he does make a request of people. Read John 5:14. What is that request?*

THE EXTRA MILE

- *How do the good things that God has done for you—
  including forgiving your sins and healing your body—
  inspire you to change your behavior? What behaviors still
  need to change? How do you plan to make those changes
  happen in your life?*

SHARE GOD'S HEART

In John 5:24, Jesus spoke about the benefits of believing in him—that is, trusting his ability and desire to save and to heal us, embracing his message and the One who had sent him in the first place: "I speak to you an eternal truth: if you embrace my message and believe in the One who sent me, you will never face condemnation, for in me, you have already passed from the realm of death into the realm of eternal life!" He offers us not only hope for this life but also for our life after death. What good news!

But Jesus went on to describe a group of people who could not seem to grasp these truths. He said this: "You are busy analyzing the Scriptures, frantically poring over them in hopes of gaining eternal life. Yet everything you read points to me, and you still refuse to come to me so that I can give you the life you're looking for—eternal life!" (vv. 39–40).

- *Many people in our world today are like this: They know a lot about Jesus, they may even know a lot about God's Word, but they don't know him for themselves. Who do you know in this situation? What do you think would help them understand Jesus' heart for them and how much he wants to touch their lives?*

- *How can you show them (not tell them about) God's love in the next week? Ask the Spirit to guide you to an answer.*

Talking It Out

1. What are some reasons people do not believe in Jesus?

2. Why might a person say they "believe in" Jesus but not follow him?

3. What are some of the benefits of believing in and following Jesus? What are some of the costs involved?

LESSON 5

Good News:
Your Needs Are Met

(6:1–71)

Have you ever noticed that for every need a human being has, there is a corresponding way to meet that need on the earth? When we find ourselves hungry, there is food to eat. When we are thirsty, there just happens to be a substance called water that will quench that thirst. We need air to breathe in order to live, and our environment contains the exact combination of oxygen, carbon dioxide, and other gases that we need to survive and thrive.

It's almost as if someone planned it that way.

If our Creator has been meeting our needs since the very day he thought up the idea of human beings, why would we think that he has no interest in really seeing that our needs are met now? Why would we think that he doesn't care?

Many people think their everyday worries are beneath the interest of the Lord of the universe. But God is interested in every detail of our lives. And he sent Jesus to prove it to us.

We Need Provision: Jesus Multiplies Food for the Crowds

When Jesus was out preaching to a huge crowd of people (five thousand men, not including women and children), the realization came to his disciples that the people were getting hungry—and back then, there was no local McDonald's on the corner that could serve up burgers and fries for that many people on such short notice. They had a pretty big problem on their hands. Jesus brought it to his disciples' attention.

- *Read John 6:5–6. What is the question Jesus asked of Philip, and why did he ask it?*

- *If Jesus had asked you this question in this situation, how would you have responded?*

- *Are you facing an "impossible" situation in your life right now? Most of us do at one time or another. Describe it. Realistically speaking, without God's intervention, what would be the likely result?*

- *Philip hadn't yet reached the deep realization of what Jesus was capable of in the most challenging situations. You know more about Jesus than Philip did back then. How can you better take your eyes off of your situation and instead put them on Jesus? What is he capable of in your situation?*

Even when Philip's faith began to grow, his expectation was still at "snack level" (v. 7). But when Jesus got involved, he fed the entire crowd—and everyone had as much food as they wanted (v. 11).

- *When it comes to trusting in Jesus to meet the needs you are facing today, are you at "snack level" or "eat till you are satisfied level"?*

- *Jesus went over and beyond in his generous response to the hungry crowds of people. In what ways has he been overly generous to you?*

We Need Safety: Jesus Walks on Water

The disciples were out on the lake—and in the middle of a storm. It was a precarious situation. The situation could have seemed much worse when what looked like a ghost came walking toward them—on top of the water. Thankfully it was no ghost but rather a very real Jesus performing yet another very real miracle.

When Jesus got to where his followers were huddled in the boat, he offered them immediate reassurance: "Don't be afraid. You know who I am" (6:20).

- *What fears and insecurities do you face? They might be less tangible than actual waves crashing against a boat, but they still impact you and need to be addressed.*

- *How does knowing Jesus calm your fears?*

We Need Eternal Life: Jesus Is the Living Bread

Yes, Jesus promises to meet our needs and calm our fears in this life—but that will only help us until the day we eventually pass away and leave this earth. What happens then?

The truth is that this life is not all there is. We are offered eternal life with God in heaven when we trust in Jesus to save us from sin and death. When we allow him to work in our lives and we turn from sin, we know that even though we will one day die a physical death, our spirit—the inner person who lives within our body—will live forever.

- Read John 6:35, 48–50. Why do you think Jesus called himself the "Bread of Life"?

- What can this Bread do for you? What must you do to receive these blessings?

EXPERIENCE GOD'S HEART

The relationship you have with Jesus can and should be the most intimate and personal relationship you experience in life. He is the One who knows you the best and who loves you the most.

- How easy or difficult is it for you to experience intimacy with Jesus? What might be standing in your way?

- *In John 6:37, Jesus declares, "All who come to me, I will embrace and will never turn them away." Picture Jesus pulling you into an embrace. What thoughts cross your mind? What emotions do you feel?*

- *How can you show your love to Jesus in return?*

- *Jesus continues this thought in John 6:40, including the Father's perspective: "The longing of my Father is that everyone who embraces the Son and believes in him will experience eternal life." What does it mean for you to realize that God longs to usher you into his kingdom to live with him forever? How does it change your perspective on this life in the here and now?*

 SHARE GOD'S HEART

Despite Jesus' immense love for every human being and despite the longing of the Father for every person to join him in everlasting life, the fact remains that not everyone will believe in Jesus and receive this free gift. Jesus recognized this and pointed it out:

> "The Holy Spirit is the one who gives life, that which is of the natural is no help. The words I speak to you are Spirit and life. But there are still some of you who won't believe." In fact, Jesus already knew from the beginning who the skeptics were. (vv. 63–64)

- *It is the Holy Spirit's job, not ours, to draw people to Christ. Our job is simply to be a witness of Christ. Have you ever tried to do this job of the Holy Spirit's for him? What was the result?*

- *Who are the doubters and skeptics that you know in your own life? How can you continue to share Jesus and his love with them, even as they continue to doubt or even outright refuse to believe?*

Despite the doubters, there are still people like Peter in the world, people who are willing to loudly declare to Jesus: "We're fully convinced that you are the Anointed One, the Son of the Living God, and we believe in you!" (v. 69).

- *That was Peter's declaration of faith. Write yours here.*

- *How can you live that declaration out in front of others over the next week?*

Talking It Out

1. Some believers think the church should meet the physical needs of people before offering them spiritual answers. Others see spiritual needs as more important than physical needs. How do you see the interplay between meeting people's physical and spiritual needs?

2. What was Jesus' response to this dilemma?

3. What should our response be?

4. Whose needs—physical, spiritual, or both—could you help to meet this week?

LESSON 6

Good News: You Are Forgiven

(7:1–8:59)

Have you ever been caught?

- Hand in the cookie jar
- Speeding in front of a cop with a radar gun
- Gossiping about someone who overhears your conversation

There comes that sinking feeling of guilt and shame—of knowing you are the only one to blame and there is nowhere to hide.

The religious leaders of Jesus' day created just such a situation for a woman who had committed one of the most heinous sins in that society: adultery. Jesus once again shows us the heart of the Father in how he responds to her—and he responds to us in the very same way.

Divided Opinions

Jesus was clear about his own mission and purpose on earth. Read his words in John 7:28–29. He was sent to show us the Father's heart.

Nevertheless, Jesus was—and still is—a controversial figure. Religion and politics aren't just hot topics for our generation. They have been dividing people for thousands of years. Back in Jesus' day, the crowd was full of different opinions about him:

> When the crowd heard Jesus' words, some said, "The man really is a prophet!" Others said, "He's the Messiah!" But others said, "How could he be the Anointed One?" . . . So the crowd was divided over Jesus. (John 7:40–43)

• *What are some of the positions people take today about who Jesus is?*

• *What is your position? Write it out here.*

The Adulterous Woman Forgiven

The woman who was dragged before Jesus was all alone in her humiliation even though she was being accused of a sin that would obviously involve more than just her. (It does take "two to tango," after all.)

- *It's purely conjecture, but where do you think her adulterous lover was? Why do you think he would not have also been dragged in front of the crowd?*

- *Have you ever been called out and shamed in a public manner for something you have done? Was the accusation fair? How did it feel?*

Likely some other men in the crowd of accusers had also committed adultery, maybe not with this particular woman but probably with someone else. Even if they had not committed this moral wrong, they were still all sinners in the eyes of a holy God.

- *What do you think is the significance of Jesus' leaning down and writing in the dust rather than responding to the woman's accusers verbally?*

- *What words do you think he wrote? Consider the notes in The Passion Translation for John 8:6, 7, and 8.*

Whatever he wrote, everybody there dropped their stones and left until only Jesus and the woman remained. And that is when something truly beautiful occurred. Through gasps of what had to be an immense sense of relief, the woman looked up and saw . . . Jesus. She saw him for who he really was. And she called him "Lord" (8:11).

> The Aramaic contains a powerful testimony from this woman. Apparently the woman had the revelation of who Jesus really was, for she addressed Jesus with the divine name in the Aramaic, *MarYah*, Lord Yahweh![10]

 EXPERIENCE GOD'S HEART

- *Write out Jesus' words found in John 8:11.*

- *Are there any sins that, while you may have asked Jesus for forgiveness, still bring you a sense of condemnation and guilt? List them here.*

- *Now imagine Jesus speaking the words of John 8:11 to you. What does his statement mean to you? Consider what impact it can have on how you view yourself and your relationship to God.*

♥ SHARE GOD'S HEART

Jesus' words immediately following his encounter with the adulteress in John 8 tell us more about his mission on the earth: "Then Jesus said: 'I am light to the world and those who embrace me will experience life-giving light, and they will never walk in darkness'" (v. 12).

- *Moral and spiritual darkness is found in all sorts of places and situations in our world today. Who do you know who is living life in the dark today?*

- *How can you be a light in that darkness?*

 WORD WEALTH

A key verse in John 8 is, "So if the Son sets you free from sin, then become a true son and be unquestionably free!" (v. 36).

- *What does it mean to be a slave to sin?*

- *Addiction can be a powerful, even deadly, condition in people's lives that can leave them feeling helpless and enslaved. What things have you been addicted to throughout the course of your life? Have you overcome those addictions? If so, how?*

- *Who in your life needs to be set free from the bondage of sin? How can you be a help to them today?*

Talking It Out

1. Read John 7:11–36, 40–43. List as many different reactions that people had to Jesus as you can from these verses.

2. Do you see any of these same reactions to Jesus today? In whom? What do these people say?

3. What would you say in response to these people and their reactions to the Savior?

4. Now read John 7:46. What "amazing things" has Jesus spoken to you? To the world?

LESSON 7

When Bad Things Happen

(9:1–10:42)

Many people find it difficult to trust in God when bad things happen. They feel the need to understand the "why" behind what takes place. But answering the "why" question isn't always easy.

Most of us, if we are honest, struggle when we can't figure out why God allows certain things to take place, especially if they are uncomfortable or difficult. But we don't seem to wonder how unfair life is when good things happen to us that we don't deserve.

The blind man Jesus encountered faced these very issues, and while his story doesn't give us the answer to the age-old question of why bad things happen to good people, it does remind us that Jesus is intimately connected with our experiences. He knew us long before we were woven together in our mother's womb, and he knows each challenge we will ever face throughout our lifetimes. Even if some of our questions remain unanswered, we can safely trust in him to guide our steps and lead us through even the most difficult situations.

The Man Born Blind

Our Lord performed miracles in order
to meet human needs. But He also used
those miracles as a "launching pad" for a
message conveying spiritual truth. Finally,
His miracles were His "credentials" to
prove that He was indeed the Messiah.
"The blind receive their sight" was one
such messianic miracle (Matt. 11:5), and we
see it demonstrated in John 9.[11]

When Jesus noticed a man on the street who had been blind
from birth, his disciples brought up the ever-honest but ever-
controversial question that we often think about but don't say
aloud when we see someone struggling with a difficult situation:
"Teacher, whose sin caused this guy's blindness, his own, or the
sin of his parents?" (John 9:2).

Notice that their assumption was negative right off the bat.
They presumed that it was sin that had caused the man's blindness. Their only question at this point was: Whose sin was it?

- *Why do you think we often approach God with such
  negative mindsets?*

- *What negative mindsets do you find it hard to break free from in your relationship with God? How does Jesus' example of what the Father is like help you shatter these ideas?*

Jesus answered his disciples: Nobody's sin caused the blindness! Their minds must have been blown.

- *What was the reason for the blindness that Jesus gave in John 9:3?*

- *Does Jesus' statement and subsequent healing of the man affect your thinking about why bad things happen to good people? If so, in what ways?*

When Jesus healed the man, it caused a bit of a commotion.

- *What were some of the reactions the people had when they saw the man after his healing had taken place? (vv. 6–9.)*

- *What was the man's response to their astonishment (vv. 10–11)?*

The man was so transformed by Jesus that people who knew him well didn't even recognize him!

- *Is there anyone you know who has been this radically transformed by an encounter with Jesus? Maybe it's you! Tell the story.*

- *What kind of transformation is God currently working in your life? In what ways would you like people (even those who know you well) to someday not even recognize you?*

- *How can you help God in the transformational process?*

EXPERIENCE GOD'S HEART

Unfortunately, there were people in the crowds who missed out on the joy of the blind man's healing because they were so caught up in the "rules" of the Sabbath that they believed Jesus was breaking.

- *What part do rules—even the commandments of Scripture—play in your relationship with God?*

- *When you break a rule, what happens? What do you usually do? What is God's response to you?*

- *Has legalism ever hindered your relationship with God? If so, how? What did you do about it, if anything?*

- *How can you move beyond the strict boundaries of the letter of the law and get to the heart of God that Jesus came to reveal?*

♥ SHARE GOD'S HEART

When the religious leaders and other accusers of Jesus approached the man who had been healed of blindness, they demanded, "Swear to God to tell us the truth! We know the man who healed you is a sinful man! Do you agree?" (9:24). But the man replied, "I have no idea what kind of man he is. All I know is that I was blind and now I can see for the first time in my life!" (v. 25).

- *In our world today, most people are interested in results. How does the healed man's response here reflect that interest?*

The healed man had quite a story to tell. Read his words in John 9:30–33.

- *The healing made the difference for this man's ability to believe in Jesus as God. What's your story? What made the difference for you when you first believed?*

- *What elements of your transformed life can you share that might make a difference in the life of someone else?*

As we have mentioned before, some people will choose not to believe for one reason or another. Read in John 9:15–17 and 26–41 some of the Jewish leaders' reactions to the healed blind man's account of what happened to him and how Jesus handled his critics and the former blind man.

- *What are we to do with people who criticize Jesus? What would have been your response?*

- *Jesus responded to more of the religious leaders' objections and criticism later, in John 10. Summarize Jesus' reasoning found in verses 25–38.*

- *What evidence has convinced you that Jesus is in the Father and the Father is in him?*

Talking It Out

1. Which is more important in the passage in the Gospel of John we have just considered: physical sight or spiritual sight? Of these two, which did Jesus emphasize?

2. Why do you think Jesus went through the process of making mud, putting it on the blind man's eyes, and then instructing him to go wash it off, rather than just healing him immediately? What point was Jesus making?

3. How do Christians today react as the Pharisees reacted to this miracle? How do they react as the neighbors did? As the healed man himself?

4. What disability or weakness do you have in your life through which you have seen God receive glory? Tell what happened.

LESSON 8

Resurrection Life

(11:1–54)

Ever since Adam and Eve ate of the forbidden fruit in the Garden of Eden, death has plagued the human race. It is the ultimate separation from our loved ones—and without Jesus' sacrifice, it would bring about the ultimate separation from God for all of eternity.

The situation grieved the Father. We know this because of Jesus' reaction when his good friend Lazarus died. Jesus wept at his gravesite—even though he knew Lazarus would walk out of the tomb just a short time later. The sting of death and the grief that his friends and all people feel when their cherished loved ones take their final breaths on this earth touched Jesus.

Jesus came to put an end to the sting of death once and for all—through his own death and resurrection. When his friend Lazarus became ill and died, though, Jesus took the opportunity to share a taste of what God the Father desires for all of his people: Life! Health! Joy!

"The One You Love"

John 11 tells the story of Jesus' close friends—the sisters Mary and Martha and their brother Lazarus. Jesus loved to spend time with this family; they were some of his most intimate companions outside of the followers he had chosen to travel with him.

So it had to have been troubling to Jesus when he received word that Lazarus had fallen ill. It was not a sickness that Lazarus would recover from either; he was at death's door. Mary and Martha were likely frantic when they sent word to Jesus to come right away: "Lord, our brother Lazarus, the one you love, is very sick. Please come!" (v. 3).

Consider the words they chose to send. They knew that Jesus could help. They called him "Lord," after all. And they weren't asking him to come to simply hold their hands. They believed that Jesus could do something to intervene in the situation.

Notice too that they knew Jesus cared. They referred to Lazarus as "the one you love." They assumed that because Jesus cared and because he had the power to help, things would be okay.

And then Lazarus died.

- *Has this ever happened to you? Have you believed for something, been sure God could do it, and believed he loved you enough to give it to you—only to see the situation fall apart? Tell the story.*

- *Did this affect your trust in God? If so, in what ways?*

- *Do you know the end of your story yet? If not, how would you like God to intervene? If he chooses to respond differently, how might you respond to him?*

Lazarus "Falls Asleep"

In John 11:11–12, Jesus uses the euphemism that Lazarus had fallen asleep. The people around him didn't understand that he was referring to the fact that Lazarus had just died. In retrospect, in the light of Jesus finally raising Lazarus from the grave, today we can see that death is really more like falling asleep than anything else—and waking up in the presence of the Lord.

Still, in case there was any doubt that Lazarus was in fact dead, Jesus made this clear in John 11:14, and later on we read that Lazarus had been in the tomb for four days before Jesus even arrived; his body was already decomposing.

Imagine the creative miracle that would have to take place for Lazarus to come walking out alive!

- *Before he took the trip to Bethany, Jesus called the situation an "opportunity to . . . learn to trust" in him (v. 15). What opportunities have you been given throughout your life to learn to trust in Jesus? What were some of the lessons you learned through those opportunities? How did your relationship with Jesus grow as a result?*

 THE EXTRA MILE

- *What opportunities do you currently have to learn to trust in Jesus more? What can you do to take advantage of those opportunities?*

 EXPERIENCE GOD'S HEART

When Jesus actually arrived, the sisters, Mary and Martha, were heartbroken at the loss of their beloved brother. Martha's initial response to Jesus shows her disappointment:

> Martha said to Jesus, "My Lord, if only you had come sooner, my brother wouldn't have died. But I know that if you were to ask God for anything, he would do it for you." (vv. 21–22)

- *Notice Martha's words: "If only you had come sooner." What if-onlys do you have in your life that reflect your disappointment in the way things have turned out?*

- *Martha took her if-only straight to Jesus. Do the same here by writing a prayer that expresses your feelings to the Lord about the disappointments you have faced.*

- *Despite her sadness, grief, and disappointment, Martha still declared her belief in Jesus at the end of verse 21. Note her words "But I know." What do you know about God that sees you through the tough times in your life?*

- *Jesus explained to Martha that he was there to bring life to Lazarus and to the rest of the world. His key question is important to all of us: "Do you believe this?" (v. 26). What about you? Do you believe this? Why or why not?*

SHARE GOD'S HEART

- *Martha's immediate response when she grasped what Jesus was saying was to run and find her sister, Mary. This was the most exciting news she could have ever dreamed of! What were the words she whispered to Mary (read verse 28)?*

- *Imagine someone whispering those very words to you: "The Master is here and he's asking for you." How would you respond? What emotions would run through your heart?*

The words "The Master is here" carry amazing implications not only for us but also for the entire world. Jesus is *Immanuel*— God with us. He is here. He is present in every situation you face.

- *Let that realization sink in. How does the presence of Jesus with you make a difference?*

- *Martha whispered to her sister that Jesus had arrived. How can you alert the people around you who need to know that he is here for them too? How might it make a difference in their lives?*

THE EXTRA MILE

- *After Mary understood that Jesus had actually arrived, she ran to find him, and people in turn followed her. She led to Jesus crowds of people who wept at their pain. What were their reactions to Jesus' arrival? (Read John 11:36–37.)*

- *Imagine the people in your world who might react these ways to Jesus. How could you respond to each of these reactions in these people whom you know?*

Grief and Grace

As a human being, and also as the One who came to show us what God the Father is like, Jesus had intense emotions. These emotions were on full display at the tomb of Lazarus (v. 38).

The truth is: Jesus feels your pain. Jesus is with you in your grief. And Jesus takes action.

He shouted with authority, using the power the Father had given him on this earth to make a difference in the situation. He came to heal, not to destroy (v. 42).

And Lazarus walked out of the tomb. What a story he likely could have told!

Jesus himself would be facing the same situation—death and resurrection—just a short time later.

- *Read John 11:52. Whom was Jesus' death meant to save?*

- *What does it mean to you that you are one of the people who was "scattered around the world" but who was brought near by Jesus to receive his love and grace? Write a prayer here expressing your thoughts and emotions to the Lord.*

Talking It Out

1. When Jesus received word that his dear friend Lazarus was sick, he was about a one-day journey away from Lazarus and his family—if he hurried. Imagine yourself as one of the disciples who heard Jesus give an encouraging message rather than leaving immediately to go to his friends' side. What would your reaction have been?

2. How did Jesus not meet the expectations of his friends and followers in this situation? How does this relate to our own expectations of God's healing and alleviation of suffering in the Christian life?

3. How does Jesus' weeping at the grave of Lazarus demonstrate his care and concern for our suffering, even when our expectations are not met? How does this speak to his love for you personally?

LESSON 9

Our Triumphant King

(11:55–12:50)

Have you ever felt rejected? Misunderstood? Despised despite all of the good you try to do for the people around you? People whom you love deeply but who do not love you in return?

If so, you know how Jesus felt as his life on this earth was coming to an end. He was met with hostility more and more wherever he traveled; in some places, it had risen to a fever pitch. People expressed opposition and hatred more violently by the day.

Perhaps the greatest burden, though, was the knowledge that he was about to face his true mission: saving the human race from sin through a brutal death on the cross. Jesus, the true King of the universe, was to willingly set aside his status as royalty, take on the role of a servant, and give up his very life for the people whom he loved so dearly.

Jesus would choose the way of the cross, ultimately dying with a crown of thorns on his head rather than a crown of jewels, but he would rise triumphant over death and the grave and rule as our triumphant King.

This chapter gives us a glimpse of him as this royal King prepares to face his ultimate mission on the earth.

Anointed by Mary

Mary, the sister of Lazarus, whom Jesus had raised from the dead, loved Jesus passionately. She had listened, enraptured at his teachings, and had seen him call her beloved brother out from the grave. Jesus' heart was likely heavy as his upcoming death loomed near, and Mary may have sensed this grief in his spirit. She took out her best bottle of perfume and poured it over his feet, anointing him with an oil that was normally reserved for the royalty among the kings of Israel. The lingering scent likely followed Jesus throughout his upcoming trial and crucifixion.

- *What do you think Mary's act of love brought to mind for Jesus himself?*

- *What might the scent of the perfume have brought to mind for Jesus' accusers at his trial?*

- *What does it mean to you that the very ones he had created and rightly ruled turned over the King of the universe for execution?*

- *Mary was not aware that she was actually anointing the King for his burial. What do you think her motivation was in this act of love she offered the Savior?*

 THE EXTRA MILE

- *What is the costliest gift you have ever offered to God? Maybe it was one of your possessions, or maybe it was a sacrifice of obedience, doing something he had asked you to do even though it was very difficult.*

- *Why did you give this gift to God? What prompted it?*

- *What was the result, not just in the situation but also in your ongoing relationship with God?*

The Triumphant Entry to Jerusalem

When Jesus entered into the city of Jerusalem for his last Passover meal before his death, throngs of cheering people greeted him, waving palm branches and shouting his praises.

- *What phrase were the people crying out as Jesus entered the city? (Read John 12:13.)*

The people likely chose to wave palm branches in praise of Jesus because such branches were convenient, but they do have special meaning, indicating his upcoming victory over death and the grave.

> The palm tree is a symbol of triumph,
> victory over death. Palms grow in the
> desert and overcome the arid climate.
> Deborah sat under a palm tree as a judge
> in Israel and received the strategy to
> overcome her enemies.[12]

- *What ordinary objects do you have around you that you could use to bring praise to the triumphant King?*

When Jesus saw the crowds of people waving the palm branches and shouting his praises, he was likely reminded of his upcoming victory-over-death mission. Another reminder to Jesus of his mission was how he entered the city: namely, riding on a donkey. By coming into the city of Jerusalem in this manner, rather than in a kingly procession filled with golden chariots, he fulfilled the prophecy found in Zechariah 9:9. He is our triumphant King, but he chose to humble himself on our behalf.

- *How does Jesus' humility speak to you? What does it say about his true mission on the earth?*

DIGGING DEEPER

Judas Iscariot

Aside from satan himself, Judas Iscariot is likely the most hated character in all of the Scriptures. The man who ultimately betrayed Jesus was someone who had been chosen by the Lord to be one of his closest friends, a member of his inner circle of twelve followers with whom he would spend three years of life and ministry. And yet Jesus knew Judas would eventually betray him. Jesus indicated this foreknowledge at the Passover supper he shared with his friends when he dipped his bread into the cup and handed it to Judas.

Judas's moniker "Iscariot" actually indicates that he was a locksmith of sorts. We know he was the treasurer in Jesus' band of friends, so he likely held a box of money that was locked in some fashion. The Bible tells us that he was a thief, out to gain fortune for himself by stealing from Jesus' funds. And Judas was the one who objected in an earlier chapter when Mary, Lazarus's sister, anointed Jesus' feet with a bottle of costly perfume.

Whatever else might be known or unknown about Judas Iscariot, one thing is clear: He was far more concerned with earthly wealth and treasure than he was about his fellow human beings or Jesus' true mission. He later betrayed Jesus for money in the garden of Gethsemane, but at some point he realized that money would not satisfy his deepest needs, and he ultimately took his own life in despair.

- *Have you ever been consumed by the pursuit of wealth the way that Judas was? If so, what changed you?*

- *Have you ever known anyone who was completely blinded to the truth by the love of money? How can the love of money distort a person's sense of values?*

- *How can we break free of the love of money before it ultimately destroys us?*

Voice from the Sky

Jesus' purpose on earth wasn't clear to his disciples even after years spent together listening to his teaching and watching his miracles. But Jesus knew that his time to die was fast approaching, so he tried to make things clear. He told a story about a grain of wheat that was dropped into the ground and died but which later sprouted and brought forth a great harvest. He went on to say:

> "The person who loves his life and pampers himself will miss true life! But the one who detaches his life from this world and abandons

himself to me, will find true life and enjoy it forever! If you want to be my disciple, follow me and you will go where I am going. And if you truly follow me as my disciple, the Father will shower his favor upon your life." (John 12:25–26)

- *Are you someone who loves your life and pampers yourself? Or are you someone who detaches your life from the world and abandons yourself to Christ?*

- *Most of us fall somewhere between these two options. In what ways can you move yourself further toward Christ and away from the world this week? List three ways in which you "pamper yourself" that keep you tied to the world that you would be willing to give up in order to experience more of Jesus in your life.*

# EXPERIENCE GOD'S HEART

As he faced his impending death upon the cross, Jesus was deeply grieved. The Scriptures tell us that his soul was in turmoil. During his time of extreme need, a voice boomed from heaven, reminding him of his ultimate purpose and helping him to maintain his focus on the end goal: redeeming mankind (read John 12:27–30). But Jesus didn't just take the words from heaven for himself; he told the people around him that it was to help them believe as well.

- *When was the last time you were so deeply grieved that your soul was in turmoil? What was happening in your life at that time?*

- *How did God speak to you in the midst of your pain?*

- *Did the people around you see God working in the midst of that situation? If so, in what ways?*

🌑 SHARE GOD'S HEART

Jesus came to share the love of the Father with every person he could reach. But no matter how loving, compassionate, and full of grace and truth that Jesus was, some people in the crowds still "refused to believe" (v. 37).

Still others whom Jesus encountered believed, but they "kept it secret" (vv. 42–43).

- *What is the most unusual reaction you have seen someone have toward Jesus' love and compassion extending toward him or her?*

No matter what people's reactions are to the message of Jesus and God's love, we are still asked to share what he has done for us.

> Jesus shouted out passionately, "To believe in me is to also believe in God who sent me. For when you look at me you are seeing the One who sent me. I have come as a light to shine in this dark world so that all who trust in me will no longer wander in darkness." (vv. 44–46)

- *When have you wandered in darkness?*

- *How did the light of Jesus' love save you?*

- *To whom can you share that light this week? How do you plan to do so?*

Talking It Out

1. Read John 12:25–26. What apparently conflicting approaches to life does Jesus mention?

2. How does Jesus' way of living run contrary to what we tend to believe is true, even today?

3. Reread verse 26. What does it mean to truly follow Jesus? How have you followed him in your own life, and what has been the result?

4. Christians through the ages have followed Jesus, many leading lives that have inspired others to grow more deeply in their relationship to God and service for him. Discuss one or more of these individuals from the past or the present who have influenced you to draw closer to God and live more consistently for him.

LESSON 10

Preparing for Death

(13:1–17:26)

The very same God who created the universe bowed down to wash the feet of sinful people. Jesus, the Son of God, who gave up the riches of heaven to show us what the Father was like, picked up a towel and a basin and took the most humble of positions in the room.

In a similar way, the triumphant King, whom throngs of people praised as he entered the holy city at the beginning of the week, was preparing to die a brutal death as crowds of people now cursed his name and called for his execution.

Jesus faced these ironies head-on as he prepared himself for his upcoming death. The Sinless One would take on the sins of the world. God himself would offer up his life to save his people from eternal death. What great love the Father has showered on us through the gift of his Son!

Washing the Feet of His Friends

Jesus had showed "deep" and "tender" love as he led his disciples through the previous three years of life and ministry. He continued to show this love for them as he knelt before them to wash their feet.

• *What feelings do you think the disciples experienced when they watched Jesus, their master and Lord, take on the most humble role of all and begin to wash the dust from their feet?*

As was typical of Simon Peter, his reaction was extreme:

> Peter did not understand what his Lord was doing, but instead of waiting for an explanation, he impulsively tried to tell the Lord what to do. There is a strong double negative in John 13:8. The Greek scholar Kenneth Wuest translated Peter's statement: "You shall by no means wash my feet, no, never." Peter really meant it! Then when he discovered that to refuse the Lord would mean to lose the Lord's fellowship, he went in the opposite direction and asked for a complete bath![13]

• *What do you think your reaction would have been if you were one of the disciples in the room? Why would you have responded in this way?*

- *How do you wash the feet of other people in your day-to-day life?*

THE EXTRA MILE

- *How can you make a more conscious effort to serve other people? They may not need their feet washed, but there are plenty of dirty jobs that still need to be done. Whom can you surprise with an act of service today?*

Predicting the Betrayal of His Friends

Jesus knew that two of those in his most intimate circle of friends were about to turn their backs on him: Judas and Simon Peter.

- *Jesus called out Judas at the Passover table, dipping his piece of bread and then handing it to Judas, alerting his friend that he knew what Judas was planning to do. How might Judas have felt, being called out like this?*

- *How might Jesus have felt as he handed the piece of bread to Judas Iscariot, knowing what was about to happen?*

Peter took a rather self-righteous stance when the topic of betrayal came up, insisting that he would never deny the Lord in such a way. Unfortunately, the very thing he bragged he would not do, he actually did—and just a short time later.

- *Have you ever bragged about something only to trip up in that very area not long afterward? Tell the story.*

- *How might Jesus have felt as he corrected Peter and foreshadowed how Peter would soon deny that he even knew Jesus?*

- *Peter was confronted with the reality of his betrayal of Jesus. How solid is your commitment? If it came down to it, what would you be willing to risk for self-identifying as a follower of Jesus? Your job? Your financial status? Your social standing? Your relationships with friends or family members? Examine your heart and write out your thoughts.*

Jesus' Last Words to His Friends

Jesus wanted to offer comfort to those closest to him in the light of what was about to happen. He shared with them good news about the mansions that awaited them in the heavenly kingdom, about the coming of the Holy Spirit after Jesus had ascended to the Father, and then he gave them what is arguably the greatest command in the entire Bible:

"So this is my command: Love each other deeply, as much as I have loved you. For the greatest love of all is a love that sacrifices all. And this great love is demonstrated when a person sacrifices his life for his friends." (John 15:12–13)

- *Who in your life has sacrificed for you? In what ways did they make a sacrifice that was meaningful to you?*

- *What did this sacrifice teach you about love?*

- *What does this sacrifice show you about God's love for you?*

⚘ EXPERIENCE GOD'S HEART

In John 17, just before Jesus would be arrested, tried, and sentenced to death, he took the time to offer up a prayer to his Father in heaven—first for his disciples at that time and then for you. Yes, for *you*. Jesus prayed for the believers who would come long after he had left this earth, and that includes you and me—if we count ourselves among those who have trusted in Jesus and what he has done for us.

Let's take a look at this prayer that Jesus prayed specifically for us:

> "And I ask not only for these disciples, but also for all those who will one day believe in me through their message. I pray for them all to be joined together as one even as you and I, Father, are joined together as one. I pray for them to become one with us so that the world will recognize that you sent me . . . You live fully in me and now I live fully in them so that they will experience perfect unity, and the world will be convinced that you have sent me, for they will see that you love each one of them with the same passionate love that you have for me. Father, I ask that you allow everyone that you have given to me to be with me where I am! Then they will see my full glory—the very splendor you have placed upon me because you have loved me even before the beginning of time . . . All those who believe in me also know that you have sent me! I have revealed to them who you are and I will continue to make you even more real to them, so that they may experience the same endless love that you have for me, for your love will now live in them, even as I live in them!" (17:20–26)

- *Write a prayer here in response to Jesus' prayer for you. Express your thoughts and emotions as you consider his passionate love for you.*

♥ SHARE GOD'S HEART

In Jesus' prayer for you, he revealed an important key to sharing God's love with the world: "The world will be convinced that you have sent me, for they will see that you love each one of them with the same passionate love that you have for me" (v. 23).

- *What will convince people of the truth?*

- *In what ways have you shown God's passionate love to fellow believers?*

- *What can you do this week to continue to demonstrate this love to God's people?*

Talking It Out

1. Later in the Bible, the same author of the Gospel of John writes in 1 John 3:16, "This is how we have discovered love's reality: Jesus sacrificed his life for us. Because of this great love, we should be willing to lay down our lives for one another." He continues in verse 17: "If anyone sees a fellow believer in need and has the means to help him, yet shows no pity and closes his heart against him, how is it even possible that God's love lives in him?" How do these two verses relate to one another?

2. Often, living for Jesus from day to day is much harder than the ultimate sacrifice of physically dying for him. In what ways do you die to self every day as you choose to live for him?

3. Does your "dying to self" demonstrate to those around you that God's love lives in you? In what ways? What has been the result?

LESSON 11

The Greatest News of All

(18:1–20:31)

Jesus knew what was going on. He was fully in control as he faced his death in obedience to the Father's will. He accepted his fate, which included the greatest suffering any human being has ever experienced before or since. Not only did he face the excruciating physical death of crucifixion, but he also faced the spiritual death of separation from the Father as the weight of our sins pressed down upon him. Jesus was a fully innocent man, yet he took on the world's guilt. No one has ever borne such a weight.

And Jesus did all of this willingly. He went to the cross out of love. And that love—the strongest force in the universe—ultimately propelled him out of the grave and into the glorious light of resurrection. Jesus defeated not only sin and suffering but also death and the grave, opening up access to the Father for any of us who chooses to trust in him.

The Garden of Gethsemane

Jesus led his shrinking group of friends to the place where he knew he would be betrayed by Judas and then arrested. And when the soldiers and temple police came to arrest him, he offered up himself, letting them know he was the man whom they were seeking.

- *Read John 18:4–6. How did Jesus describe himself? Which Old Testament term did he use?*

- *What was the impact on the people around him when he spoke that phrase?*

- *Jesus—the great I AM—willingly gave himself over to his fate. How does his voluntary sacrifice impact your life?*

- *In what ways do you willingly serve your Savior in return for what he has done for you?*

Jesus' Trial

Jesus faced the longest night of his life. He was dragged before ruler after ruler, falsely accused, struck in the face, beaten, derided, mocked, and flogged.

- *Can you relate to any of Jesus' experiences on this, his longest night? Have you ever been unjustly accused? Bullied? Made fun of? Describe it. How did it make you feel?*

In your darkest hour, you can rest assured that Jesus understands the emotions you are facing, and he is with you in the depths of your despair. Whatever you may face in this life, he has faced it too. And he stands ready to help.

# DIGGING DEEPER

Jesus' discussion with Pilate is an interesting one—an exchange that echoes down through the centuries.

> Looking him over, Pilate asked him, "Are you really the king of the Jews?"
>
> Jesus replied, "Are you asking because you really want to know, or are you only asking this because others have said it about me?"
>
> Pilate responded, "Only a Jew would care about this; do I look like a Jew? It's your own people and your religious leaders that have handed you over to me. So tell me, Jesus, what have you done wrong?"
>
> Jesus looked at Pilate and said, "The royal power of my kingdom realm doesn't come from this world . . . My kingdom realm authority is not from this realm."
>
> Then Pilate responded, "Oh, so then you are a king?"
>
> "You are right." Jesus said, "I was born a King, and I have come into this world to prove what truth really is. And everyone who loves the truth will receive my words."
>
> Pilate looked at Jesus and said, "What is truth?" . . . Silence filled the room.
> (John 18:33–38)

- *How would you respond to Pilate's question, "What is truth?"*

 THE EXTRA MILE

Pilate had truth incarnate standing in front of him, and yet he didn't recognize Jesus as the truth, and he didn't seem to know what truth actually is. God's Word tells us a great deal about truth, and theologian Vernon Grounds does a fine job summarizing this for us:

> [T]he Biblical concept of truth is a complex of faithfulness, firmness, reliability, honesty, integrity and consistency. Truth is whatever in word, behavior and character is in alignment with reality, and ultimate reality is the God who in his unchanging holiness cannot contradict himself, who unalterably keeps his word, and who incarnates covenantal steadfastness. Truth is thus the antithesis of the unreal, the false, the hypocritical, the deceptive, the concealed, the unfaithful. As the uncreated Creator of the whole cosmos, God in his perfect wisdom is the source of all knowledge. And since God has chosen to reveal himself through Scripture, . . . whatever he says therein is to be embraced as truth. God being the God of truth, between his words and deeds there is absolute congruity. But because God, the perfect Person, is the God of truth, he in his Word stresses truth as something more than the agreement of its propositions with the reality of things and events. He emphasizes truth as a quality of human character, and he holds high Jesus his Son as the flawless example of grace and truth (John 1:14). Consequently God wills that we

know the truth (8:32), believe the truth (2 Thess 2:9), speak the truth (Eph 4:15) and above all live the truth (1 John 1:6).[14]

- *Pull out from this summary at least three biblical characteristics of truth that surprise you, encourage you, or inspire you. Write them down here.*

- *Are these truth traits a part of your life or of someone you know? If so, describe how they come through and what their impact is on other people.*

- *Referring to these truth traits or a few others mentioned in Grounds's summary above, ask the God of truth to help you make those traits more a part of your life and your interaction with others. Ask God to make you an even better conduit of the truth.*

"It Is Finished"

Jesus was sentenced to death, and, ultimately, the nails were hammered through his hands and his feet. He hung on the cross in agony, taking the punishment for our sins upon himself.

- *What does the picture of Jesus on the cross bring up in your heart? Express your heart to the Savior as you consider his great sacrifice for you.*

- *Finally, Jesus cried out the words, "It is finished!" at the moment of his death. What, exactly, had he completed?*

- *If the work of salvation has been finished, what exactly is there left for you to do?*

- *Many people try to continue Jesus' work of salvation, hoping to earn a place in heaven through their good works. Have you ever taken this approach? What was it that you thought would bring you into God's good graces? What was the result?*

 EXPERIENCE GOD'S HEART

The greatest news of all is that Jesus did not remain on the cross or in the tomb. He walked out of the grave three days after his brutal execution—and he still lives to this day!

- *What was Mary's response when she encountered the risen Lord? (See John 20:14–16.)*

- *What was the response of the disciples when they heard the good news? (See vv. 19–20.)*

- *What was Thomas's response? (See vv. 24–28.)*

- *What is your response?*

SHARE GOD'S HEART

According to John 20:30, "Jesus went on to do many more miraculous signs in the presence of his disciples, which are not even included in this book."

- *Jesus continues to perform miraculous signs today. Name some that he has performed in your life or in the life of someone you know.*

- *John, Jesus' close friend, chose to write a book to share the story of Jesus and how he had changed his life. What are some creative ways you can also share Jesus' impact on your life? Writing a book is one option. What are some others?*

Talking It Out

1. Jesus was speaking of us today when he spoke the words in John 20:29: "There are those who have never seen me with their eyes but have believed in me with their hearts, and they will be blessed even more!" What does this blessing include for you? What does it mean to have Jesus know—and commend—your belief in him, long before you were ever born?

2. Does this realization change how you relate to Jesus and your Christian walk going forward? In what ways?

3. What do you think Jesus means when he says that future believers in him will "be blessed even more"?

4. How has such blessing been showered on your life?

LESSON 12

Restored to the Savior

(21:1-25)

Perhaps the greatest message of the Gospel of John—and of the entire Bible—is this: You are forgiven! Even if you blow it, you can be restored—again and again and again.

This is made abundantly clear in the final chapter of John's book. One of Jesus' closest friends, Simon Peter, had blown it—in a pretty spectacular way. In Jesus' hour of greatest need, Peter had essentially turned his back on the Lord, denying that he knew him. Whether it was due to fear, exhaustion, or even shock at the circumstances he was facing, Peter did what he had sworn he would never do—and he did it not just one time, not twice, but three times.

To say Peter was ashamed would be an understatement.

But then the resurrection happened. And everything changed. The tender, loving Savior took the time to not only forgive one of his closest friends but also to restore their relationship, making it stronger than ever.

Jesus, your risen Lord and Savior, is also your friend. No matter what you've done, no matter how ashamed you may be of what you've done, he longs to restore you to himself.

The Meeting on the Beach

The disciples had gone out fishing. It was a return to the familiar after their lives had been turned upside down. But when Peter realized that Jesus was waiting for them on the beach, the memories of his betrayal likely filled his mind.

- *How would you have reacted if you were Peter in this moment? Have you ever denied Jesus or done something you were so ashamed to share with him?*

- *What did Peter do in John 21:7? Why was this an extreme reaction, given the circumstances?*

- *How can you be more like Peter was in this situation—running toward Jesus rather than away from him?*

When Jesus encountered Peter on the beach, he asked him to pull in the catch of fish—something Peter was familiar with doing, something he was good at, and something that likely reminded him of the day when Jesus had called him from his nets to follow the Lord.

- *What do Jesus' instructions here say to you about his desire to restore broken people?*

- *If Jesus were speaking to you, restoring you to himself, what would he ask you to do? How would you respond?*

 EXPERIENCE GOD'S HEART

To get to the heart of the matter and to heal Peter's heart on the deepest level, Jesus asked him a series of three questions, corresponding to the three times when Peter had denied Jesus on the night of his crucifixion. Imagine Jesus asking these same questions of you. Write your answers below.

- *"Do you burn with love for me more than these?"*

- *"Do you burn with love for me?"*

- *"Do you have great affection for me?"*

- *How can you live out your answers in your actions, not just in your words?*

 THE EXTRA MILE

According to *Smith's Bible Dictionary*, there is "satisfactory evidence that he and Paul were the founders of the church at Rome and died in that city. The time and manner of the apostle's martyrdom are less certain. According to the early writers, he died at or about the same time with Paul, and in the Neronian persecution, A.D. 67, 68. All agree that he was crucified. Origen says that Peter felt himself to be unworthy to be put to death in the same manner as his Master, and was, therefore, at his request, crucified with his head downward."[15]

- *Read Jesus' unusual words to Peter in John 21:18–19. What was Jesus predicting in these verses concerning Peter's future?*

- *How would you have felt if you were Peter hearing these words from Jesus? Would you have felt fear at what the future would bring or been comforted by Jesus' confidence in your faith?*

- *How might it have emboldened you to share your faith?*

♥ SHARE GOD'S HEART

John concludes his Gospel with the following words:

I, John, am that disciple who has written these things to testify of the truth, and we know that what I've documented is accurate. Jesus did countless things that I haven't included here. And if every one of his words were written down and described one by one, I suppose that the world itself wouldn't have enough room to contain the books that would have to be written! (21:24–25)

- *What "other things" has Jesus done for you, especially during the course of this study of the Gospel of John?*

- *John wrote down the account of the things he saw Jesus do and the words he heard him speak—the impact he had on John's life and on the world. In what creative ways can you best spread the message of the gospel, the good news of Jesus and what he has done?*

Talking It Out

1. Why do you think Peter returned to his fishing nets after Jesus' crucifixion? Why might he have believed that Jesus had no more use for him?

2. Have you ever tried to restore a broken relationship? What steps did you take? What was the result?

3. Peter received Jesus' forgiveness for his previous betrayal. But when Jesus indicated to Peter that his trust in him had also been restored and that his ministry would continue, that made all the difference. No matter your past failures, God can still use you to serve him and bring glory to the Lord. How does this truth speak to you?

4. How does it help you relate to others who may have failed in their Christian walk?

Endnotes

1   "About the Passion Translation," *The Passion Translation: The New Testament with Psalms, Proverbs, and Song of Songs* (Savage, MN: BroadStreet Publishing Group, 2017), iv.

2   "Introduction," John, The Passion Translation, 575.

3   Warren Wiersbe, *Be Alive* (Colorado Springs: David C. Cook, 1986), 27–28.

4   Note on John 1:29, The Passion Translation.

5   Note on John 1:32, The Passion Translation.

6   Note on John 2:2–3, The Passion Translation.

7   Note on John 3:16, The Passion Translation.

8   Note on John 4:6–8, The Passion Translation.

9   Note on John 5:2, The Passion Translation.

10   Note on John 8:11, The Passion Translation.

11   Wiersbe, *Be Alive*, 139.

12   Note on John 12:13, The Passion Translation.

13   Warren Wiersbe, *Be Transformed* (Colorado Springs: David C. Cook, 2009), 22.

14   Vernon C. Grounds, "The Truth about Truth," *Journal of the Evangelical Theological Society* (June 1995), 220.

15   William Smith, "Martyrs," *Smith's Bible Dictionary* (Nashville: Thomas Nelson Publishers, 2004), 1803.